Tales from Shelter Rock
and Beyond

Shelter Rock

Tales from Shelter Rock

and Beyond

MAC HORTON

Published by Shelter Rock Publications
Columbia, SC

Printed by Lightning Press

Cloth ISBN: 978-1-5323-3303-3
Paperback ISBN; 978-1-5323-3304-0

Contents

Part 3: No Rock Like Shelter Rock

Part 4: Oh, the Things We Did

Part 5: Sir, Yes Sir

Part 6: Live and Learn

Preface and Acknowledgments

You are about to read a group of short stories pertaining to my life experiences growing up in Heath Springs, South Carolina. Shelter Rock Service Station (Daddy's country store) was the center of my world. It was a place where people of all races and socio economic classes could have a pack of crackers and a coke, and where opinions were shared without condemnation. It was a place where I learned that all people were interesting and worthy of being heard. Although life's journey has taken me many interesting places, in my heart, I have never been far from Shelter Rock—it's where my roots are.

Writing short stories is easy. The hard work comes when one tries to bring a book to fruition, and I can assure you that this work could not have been completed without the assistance of many people. I would like to especially thank Carol, Leslie, and Willy. I would also like to thank my dear wife Libby as none of this would be possible if not for her patience and support.

Part 1

Corporal Ward Beecher Horton

We're in the Army Now

In January of 1942 my Daddy, Ward Beecher Horton, was busy living the good life. He was single with three jobs— farming, substituting as the mailman, and working for Mr. Mosley at the service station. He drove a 1938 Chevy, which was not only the fastest car in town, but also (with a little modification) a pea thrasher. As he walked into the post office that morning, he noticed his best friend, Kenneth, intensely reading a letter which had arrived in an official looking brown envelope. "Morning Ken," Daddy said as he passed. Kenneth was expressionless and made no acknowledgement as he was fixated on the letter. Emerging from the post office, Daddy was holding an ominous brown envelope of his own. Kenneth approached him saying, "Beecher, I'm not sure but I think I just got drafted." "Me, too," Daddy replied, "I guess we're in the army now." And just like that, the good life ended. Soon Daddy would leave Heath Springs, South Carolina for the battlefields of Europe, not to return until 1945— a very different man.

Iceland

Daddy fulfilled his basic training requirements at Fort Jackson and from there went to Iceland for thirteen months where they practiced shooting, learned to snow ski, and consumed pork chops every night for supper. His rifle range Sergeant told the Lieutenant that the boys from Tennessee and South Carolina didn't need any more firing practice because they could already out-shoot the instructor, and if anyone wearing the wrong uniform got within 150 yards—they would be a dead man. Daddy told me about riding sheets of tin down the mountain so far that one would intentionally wreck because if you did not, walking back would wear you out. Once his mother sent him four small Coca-Colas. He and a buddy drank one each, and buried the remaining two for later; however, that night it snowed several feet, and they were lost forever. After hearing these cool stories, I thought what an awesome adventure the war must have been and how much fun being in the army must be. Now I realize he talked mostly about Iceland because he just didn't want to go into detail about what happened in France and Germany. Anyway, he was always very proud of the fact that he could spell—Reykjavik.

Home Away from Home

After thirteen months in Iceland, Daddy was shipped to England where his unit began staging for a beach landing in France. While in England he was befriended by the Davis family, who afforded him a taste of life much like the one he had known back in South Carolina. He could get them cheese, salt, sugar, etc., and they would reciprocate with Sunday dinner and a relaxing afternoon. They had a ten-year-old daughter named Sheila whose name he liked, and whom he remembered when his own daughter (Sheila) was born several years later. On D plus three, his unit went ashore at Normandy and fought their way north through France to a small town near the Belgium-German border—where they waited. Rumors of the wars' end were abundant, and some said they would be home for Christmas; however, on December 16 they were furiously attacked by the First SS Panzer Division followed by what was left of the entire German army. The Battle of the Bulge was on, and he found himself right in the middle of it.

The Battle of the Bulge

The battle began in the wee hours of December 16 with German soldiers parachuting behind American lines and occupying many crossroads and bridges. They were dressed in American uniforms wearing MP insignia and speaking perfect English. Disrupting communications, misdirecting reinforcements, and causing confusion in general was their mission—which they accomplished to perfection. By now, Daddy had been promoted to corporal and was responsible for men from South Carolina, Tennessee, and Ohio. They were caught totally off guard by the attack as US intelligence believed that Germany was on the verge of surrender; however, nothing could have been further from the truth. (Daddy always said the term "Army Intelligence" was an oxymoron). German officers were being shot if not successfully reaching their objectives on time, so enemy incentive for victory was off the chart, and as a result the fighting was terrible—much of it occurring in close quarters and some of it hand to hand. After three days of non-stop assaults, the tide of battle began to turn in favor of the Americans as some forward units began to break through. Casualties were high, however, with 19,000 US soldiers killed and 50,000 wounded. The German Army sustained losses of 125,000 killed, wounded or missing. Daddy only suffered a flesh wound in his left hand but considered it nothing knowing he was lucky to have survived at all.

Daddy in uniform

The War Is Over

After three days and nights of fighting near Bastogne, the German army was falling into disarray; and American units began to move east rapidly. By now, what was left of Daddy's outfit had been reassigned to General Patton's Third Army and was hell bent for Berlin. Patton instructed the forward ground units not to take prisoners but to go around them and keep pushing forward. Daddy said that so many Germans were surrendering, he felt like the POW. "There were a lot more of them than us," he said. In just a few weeks, Daddy found himself thirty miles south of Berlin without food or ammunition—they had outrun their supplies. There they would wait while the Russians took the city. This was fine with Daddy as he had seen enough and was ready to come home. He had promised the Lord that if he ever got back to Heath Springs, he would never leave—that he would go into business for himself, raise a family, and be the best man he could be, which is exactly what he did.

Part 2

Childhood Heaven

Coming Home in a Hearse

When I was born, my daddy (Beecher Horton) owned and operated Shelter Rock Service Station in Heath Springs, South Carolina. In addition to running his store, he retained his position as a substitute mailman and was also in the used car business. If you were lucky enough to know Daddy, you remember that he had a passion for the unusual and it just so happened the day I came home from the hospital, he was in possession of a hearse. Driving into the yard with Mama and me caused Granny to assume that Mama had died, and out of the house she came—distraught. Her sorrow quickly turned to anger when she learned that it was simply a misunderstanding fueled by Daddy's unusual sense of humor. My cousin, "Jim Bo," would later use that same hearse to pick up girls in Lancaster as this ride proved to be quite a chick magnet and lo and behold who but Phoebe, my future wife's older sister, would be among a group of young ladies who enjoyed an afternoon cruising in eternal comfort. As you can imagine, this juicy bit of information was stumbled upon quite by accident when Phoebe learned that her sister, Libby, was marrying me, a Hesprian, but that's another story. By the way, a Hesprian is someone from Heath Springs.

Hanging out with Wup

Wup

When I was about four years old, I got a puppy. She was a mixed breed—about two thirds Collie and one third German Shephard. Her name was Wup, and we were inseparable. Everywhere I went—she went. That dog loved me and was so protective; she once bit my friend Benny for tackling me while playing backyard football. My mother could not even put her hands on me in anger because Wup would not allow it, and if my behavior needed correcting, it would have to be done inside. Mama never worried when I was playing alone in the woods as long as she knew my dog was with me, because she could depend on Wup to take care of me. Eventually I went off to college and upon returning home for Thanksgiving found a new puppy. Mama said that when I left Wup got sick and would not eat. Mama said that she died of a broken heart.

Stitches for Me

When I was about five years old, I was sitting on the end of the bed watching my older brother and sister fight. My brother, "B," was lying across the bed on his back, and Sheila was on top of him. I was urging Sheila on, so to eliminate one of his tormentors, B kicked me from the bed. My head hit the corner of the bedpost and by the time we got to Kershaw, seeking treatment, the towel wrapped around my head was soaked in blood. Dr. McDow sewed me up using several stitches, and assured Mama that I would survive. B told our mother that he thought I was his book satchel, and that he would not have taken such action if he had realized it was me. Yeah, right!

The Best Laid Plans

One Sunday night my brother brought a date to church. I was very small, and my scheme was to hurry out the back when church was over, hide behind the driver's seat of his car and sneak a ride. I had told my mother that "B" had agreed to bring me straight home—which was a lie. He and his date got in the car, closed the doors and began to drive away. It was at this point that I realized what I was doing might actually work, and it was also the point at which I realized I had no plan for what to do next. Seeing no alternative, I popped up and said, "How about a lift home?" B was angry, but his date pointed out that one should always check the back seat of the car when it's dark. "Yes," I said, "one should always check the back seat of the car when it's dark." The lie to my mother turned out to be half true—he did take me straight home.

Chasing Santa

When my sister, Sheila, was about ten and I was about six, we devised a foolproof plan to catch Santa Clause. Our Christmas tree was located in the corner of the den, and there was a door in my bedroom through which I could see all the way to the den wall. For Santa to get to the tree, he must pass by that opening; therefore, all we had to do was never take our eyes away from the doorway and sooner or later we would see him. Sitting up in bed and using a flashlight to enhance our view, we took turns watching. With an alarm clock in bed, we rotated the watch in ten minute shifts. It would have worked too if we had not fallen asleep after about two shifts. Although we never caught a glimpse of the old man or even an elf, he made the visit because in the morning I had a new cowboy suit.

With my sister, Sheila

Mr. Pum, Granny, and Nancy

Pomalroy Robertson (Mr. Pum) was my step-grandfather. He had married Granny (Daddy's mother) sometime during the late fifties, and they lived on the Robertson Place not far from us. Mr. Pum was a carpenter by trade and working in Brunswick, Georgia, he built cabinets for ships—returning to Heath Springs only on the weekends. Nancy was his field horse, and what a horse she was—so big that I would have to stack bales of hay like steps to climb on top of her. Mr. Pum communicated using words like "GEE" and "HAW" to which she would respond by going right or left. She was very smart. My job was to bring Nancy to the garden when he was ready to plow. However, in fact, it would be Nancy bringing me to the garden—she knew the way. She also pulled a box sled to bring wood up to the house, and I loved to ride in that sled holding the reins as if I was in charge, but yet again, she knew the way.

Mr. Pum and Granny

The Good Life

Mr. Pum and Granny personified country living. Their house came complete with a rain barrel, slab pile, chicken coop, and Nancy—a working horse for plowing the garden and corn patch. Not only did they heat with wood, but they also cooked with wood which Mr. Pum was forever chopping. Some said there would be no trees in Lancaster County today if he had possessed a chain saw. Of course, there was also an outhouse, which I must confess, unnerved me a little. The truth is it was downright scary, and I was more inclined to hold it until an opportunity for indoor plumbing presented itself. When I was about four or five, Granny kept me during the day, and I spent many hours trying to catch one of their numerous cats or playing in the sunflower patch which Mr. Pum grew for chicken feed. Often I would find myself lost in imagination. Life was so different in those days—kids played in the yard, hard work was the norm, and folks were thankful for what they had. People made the best of things and put their faith in God.

Carrying Water

Granny told me about her chores as a little girl growing up on a farm. Her father worked in the cotton fields, and every afternoon Granny's task was taking him cool water to drink. She was instructed not to go through the hog pen with a bucket, for obvious reasons; however, the way around was much longer and there were briars to negotiate. Finding courage in discouragement, she ignored her father's directive and was quietly scurrying from bush to tree with her water when the swine assumed it was time to dine—the chase was on. Running as fast as she could and falling down several times, she made it to the gate where she was able to climb over. Arriving at the field and handing her daddy the bucket with just a little muddy water near the bottom, she said, "Sorry Daddy, but I lost some of it to the hogs."

Chitlins

About once a year Mr. Pum would cook chitlins. For those of you who are not accustomed to fine dining, chitlins are the intestines of a pig. Some Southerners consider them a delicacy; however, the smell of them cooking has the power to render one unconscious. Small animals would leave their homes, birds would fly north, and perfectly healthy leaves would fall from the trees when this scent permeated the air. At ground zero, the grass would turn brown and grub worms could be found dead on the surface. IT SMELLED BAD! Granny would do her visiting on cooking day and usually wind up at our house to await the all clear. I can still see Mr. Pum standing by that big black pot with a raging fire underneath stirring with a boat paddle. Who's ready for some vittles?

A Heath Springs Parade

When I was a child, Granny would tell me stories about the old days, and once she told me the story of her first automobile sighting. She was a little girl living several miles from Heath Springs when word spread through the countryside that a horseless carriage would be coming through town that afternoon. Several friends and neighbors walked to town but were disappointed to learn that the vehicle had already come and gone. The trip was not a total loss; however, as they were excited to see the tracks it had left. Now the automobile was coming back, and she was afraid. Seeking safety behind a large oak tree, she watched as it passed by. "I almost missed it," she said, "there was so much excitement, and it was going so fast, I was only able to get a quick glimpse."

Candy Galore

Most of you know by now that I grew up in the country where our closest neighbor lived almost a mile away. Trick-or-treating was a matter of getting in the Rambler, and Mama driving us to five or six houses nearby. The people knew we were coming and had special treats for us, like Mrs. Haile always gave me an apple with raisins on toothpicks for arms and legs and a marshmallow for a cap. Mr. Stitizel would give us bags of candy and Fritos. The Faulkenberrys and Reeves were just as generous, showering us with Reese Cups, Mary Janes, BB Bats, and the like, not to mention the chewing gum shaped like cigars. In my mind, if I could only get to town and visit all those houses, my candy stash would be mountainous. One Halloween I did. I visited my friend Marty, and we walked all over Heath Springs trick-or-treating; but to my surprise, my intake was significantly less than my haul at the few neighbors back in the country. My first lesson on how sometimes less can be more.

Perils of First Grade

Most of you probably never even considered how much your head can be like a butterfly screw. The bolt on a butterfly screw has wings that open so that when inserted into a hole, you can tighten the screw without having access to the other side. One day my first grade class was interrupted when it came to the attention of Miz Richardson that Ricky's head was stuck between the two back rests of his desk, and his ears were performing the same function as the wings on that butterfly screw by not allowing his head to retract from its' stuck position. Frantically, Miz Richardson called Artis, the school's janitor, as he would most likely be able to think of the best solution to free Ricky's head. "That boy shore does have his head stuck in that desk," he said, "I can't right off hand recall ever having seen a boy in such a fix." He disappeared briefly and returned with his tool box. "Appears that we're going to have to operate," Artis said. Now Ricky was pale, thinking that "operate" involved performing an ear-dectomy. Artis, with the precision of a surgeon, cut the back rest with his saw and much to the delight of Miz Richardson, freed Ricky from his predicament. Now we could get back to learning how to write our name and coloring.

Punishment at School

In the second grade, Miz Dabney taught reading in a separate building located by the side of Heath Spring's grammar school auditorium. I remember marching down the hall and around the building to arrive there. One day my friend Dru was reading about Alice and Jerry, when he came upon a passage describing an adventure they were having on the water. He read, "They paddled and paddled, but they got. . . ." Suddenly he stopped, as he was struggling with the next word. The word was "nowhere," but Dru could not get it. Finally he shouted with pride "now here!" "They paddled and paddled, but they got now here," he said. Dru was usually quicker to catch on than me, but this time, I knew the correct word was "nowhere." I began laughing at his mistake. The cornerstone of our lifelong friendship has been pointing out in the most humiliating way possible the other's mistakes. Miz Dabney was unfamiliar with this budding tradition and gave me a whipping which Dru thought was funny. I was disappointed that she did not whip him for laughing at me; however, she remained firmly committed to her decision. I think it was because his mother was a teacher, and Miz Dabney knew her. Yeah, that was it.

Horror in Church

My parents were avid church goers, and you could count on seeing the Hortons at the Heath Springs Baptist Church, not only every Sunday morning, but also on Sunday and Wednesday nights. For some reason, on this particular Sunday evening, David (Reverend Gross's son), and I decided to sit on the front row. We were ten years old and about halfway through the sermon, became restless and began to misbehave. Reverend Gross was preaching away, when all of a sudden things got mysteriously quiet. At that moment he turned to Mrs. Gross who was sitting in the choir, and said, "Mrs. Gross, would you remove David from the service?" She was more than happy to oblige and popped up from the choir loft marching down to the front row, where she snatched David up and drug him out—right down the center aisle. He was crying before they reached the vestibule, and now I could hear him screaming as she pronounced judgment and administered punishment. My mother was in the congregation, and I just knew that she would soon be coming for me. Sitting there, waiting, was more painful than any whipping could ever be. So it was at the beginning of the final hymn, I felt her hand around my arm and to the vestibule we went. By this time I had become the perfect child, and I had rededicated my life promising never to sin again and especially never to misbehave in church. The Lord did not, however, answer my prayer and I got a well-deserved whipping. Mama later declared that it was mostly David's fault and that I would not have acted that way unless influenced by someone with fewer manners.

Striving for Imperfection

In grammer school, we would have these ten word spelling tests and my friend, "Buzz," would always make a 100. The competiter in me wanted to beat Buzz, but the Mac in me just wasn't willing to put in the time. Not being perfect has pretty much been my life's attitude/ filosiphy and somehow striving for imprefection has worked four me. Have you ever heard the phrase "That's close enough for government work"—I envented it. Everyone should always do there best, but life is filled with the unperdicitable, the umexpected, and the unfoureseen so overprepation is often a resipe for failure. If you learn to exsept your faults—you might be able to turn them into strengths.

"B," the Bicycle, and the Bat

When I was about 10 years old, I got a new bicycle. It was an English bicycle with three gears and hand brakes. I loved it. "B" wanted to ride it and Mama's solution was that since it was mine, he could ride after I stopped. Problem solved—I would just never stop. Eventually I did go into the house for some water, and as I stood at the kitchen window there goes B on my bicycle, and to make matters worse he sailed on around the curve where I was not allowed to go. I was consumed with rage. With my baseball bat in hand, I proceeded about twenty yards down the road where I laid in the ditch and waited. When he came back, I leapt up slinging the bat at him as hard as I could—he dodged it. Mama witnessed the whole thing from the kitchen window and out of the house she came, stopping by the spirea bush only long enough to break off a switch. She tanned my backside all the way home. That's how I learned to share.

Route 66

In the sixties during the fall of the year, new car models were released to the public, and Daddy would take me to the Chevrolet and Ford dealerships in Lancaster for the unveilings. It was a big event in those days because everyone was excited about seeing what the new models would look like and how much they would cost. I remember seeing a yellow 1963 Corvette and fantasizing about cruising down Route 66 with the wind in my hair. The only problem was the price—the sticker read $5,063.00. I was afraid that no one could afford it, but Daddy assured me that someone could. The next time I was in Lancaster, it was gone.

Age of Enlightenment

February 9th, 1964 was a Sunday. The Hortons had just returned home from church and were about to finish lunch when Sheila announced that she would not be going to the evening prayer meeting service. "Are you sick?" asked Mama. "No," she replied, "the Beatles are going to be on Ed Sullivan tonight, and I am going to watch them." Watching TV was not an acceptable excuse to miss church; however, there was a resolve in her voice that I had never noticed before, and she seemed to be making a stand. I was anxious to see how this was going to play out since I had witnessed the failure of my brother's numerous attempts to avoid church, and I had long accepted the realization that no reason short of a life-threatening illness would move my parents from their position. She explained that this was their first American appearance and how important it was for her to see them and immediately elevated her appeal to Daddy. After some discussion the issue was still in doubt when she just flat out said that she wasn't going and that no one was going to stop her from seeing the Beatles tonight. My parents relented and said that we could all skip tonight's service. Something in my brain began to tingle as I realized what had just happened. For me, a life-changing experience had just occurred and the realization that a kid had options opened up a whole new world. From this moment forward I would make my own decisions, choose my own path, and determine my own destiny. Ironically I had been "born again" by NOT going to church, and because of Sheila's insistence on seeing the Beatles, my life for better or worse would never be the same.

You'll Shoot Your Eye Out

When I was about eleven, I got a BB gun. I was shooting everything in sight when I spotted a freshly planted cedar post. The limbs had been cut from the post and one exposed a round target with a bright red center. Perfect! Standing about 30 feet away, I drew down and shot. I hit it dead center, and now the BB was coming back. I could see it coming but did not have time to react. It hit me right between the eyes. If it had struck me ¼ inch over in either direction, it would have put my eye out; and the life I know today would not exist. Lucky that my lightning fast reflexes were yet undeveloped or the stories that you are reading today would have been written from a different point of view.

Arriving in Style

Even in the mid-sixties, arriving in style was important. My grandmother on my mother's side owned a large dairy farm in Chester County; and they had lots of farm equipment, including four or five tractors. On Sunday afternoon, all the cousins would gather at Nana Willie's house for dinner, after which we played baseball, football, etc. Sometimes we would go swimming down at the wash hole which was about a mile from her house. There were enough tractors so that the older cousins each had one to drive, and if you weren't big enough to drive, you could stand on the rear axle and hold onto the seat. Talk about arriving in style—it didn't get any better than that.

How to Lose a Horsefly

Tip number 1 for growing up in the country. If you are ever playing in an open field and are being tormented by a horsefly, don't think that you can take off running and lose him. You cannot outrun a horsefly, but you may be able to outsmart him. Stand next to a horse, shoo the fly over to him, and then take off running. If a horse is not available, a cow might work if your particular fly happens to be below average. It's all about the brains.

Daddy's Wisdom

Not long after receiving a BB gun, my privileges were taken away and, although I am not proud of the reason, here it is. As I was on the hunt that afternoon, I spied Daddy's mule about thirty feet from the corner fence post. Stealthily I positioned myself and took aim at his backside. The BB lodged in his hip. It just stuck there, and he did not even lift his head—just swished his tail. That was not the reaction I was going for so I shot him again. As I pulled the trigger a third time, Daddy appeared from nowhere. Although up to that point in my life Daddy had never whipped me, he made it crystal clear that if I ever again shot any living thing with that BB gun, he would give me one to remember—I believed him. He should have torn my ass up, but he did not. He did, however, take my BB gun; and oddly enough replaced it with a 4.10 shotgun. This might sound crazy to some of you, but he realized that for a kid like me a small shotgun was much less dangerous. I have always been blessed by his wisdom and restraint, but that time he really should have torn my ass up.

Thanks for the Gate

Election night was so much fun when I was a kid. Daddy would take me to Lancaster where we would stand on the street outside the courthouse and listen to a live radio broadcast announcing the results of each precinct. Daddy knew all the candidates as they, sooner or later, stopped by Shelter Rock Service Station to campaign or to put up their signs. Once, a candidate who had earlier insulted one of Daddy's army buddies installed a nice metal sign near the store that solicited votes and insinuated that he would never turn his back on a veteran. Daddy measured the sign and decided it would make a perfect gate for the barn, so there it served a useful purpose for many years, asking his cows for their vote and warning of the BS inside.

Anybody Got a Dime?

As a young man, Halloween was one of my favorite holidays. Sure, the free candy was great, but going to the carnival at Heath Springs High School was the real treat—everybody was there. The juniors and seniors would plan the evenings' festivities, and participation in each activity cost only a dime. There was a horror show featuring a mad scientist performing a gruesome operation, as well as a horrible rock-n-roll extravaganza. There were other activities for the little ones, such as dart throwing, ring tossing, and apple bobbing. My personal favorite was the kissing booth, where for only 10 cents you could kiss a high school girl. Finally, there was the cake walk. Those were truly the good ole days, when the community was your family, and your only worry was having enough dimes.

Limp As a Dishrag

I cannot recall but one time in my life being so scared that I got weak, and this is that time. As a twelve year old, Wup would be with me as we walked from our house to Daddy's store which involved about a two mile trek through woods and pastures, traversing several pond dams. On one such outing, Wup began to act differently as we crossed the Catfish Pond Dam. She would usually be in front of me, but now she was behind barking and stopping. I would have to call her to catch up; however, she would bark and hesitate. Now that was strange, and I felt uneasy but kept walking although being careful and moving a little more slowly. All of a sudden there in the path ahead of me was a rattlesnake, and he was open for business. Coiled and rattling, he dared me to take another step and knowing that they traveled in pairs added to my fear. That unmistakable sound (which is actually more like a hum) coupled with the way he never took his eyes off me caused me to become weak and almost unable to move. I was in between being paralyzed with fear and fainting. Finally I mustered strength to take a few steps backward, then turning around, I ran back across the dam into the safety of an open pasture. That was the only rattlesnake I ever saw on the whole place, but when it comes to rattlesnakes, one is enough. And by the way, that would not be the last time Wup would save my life.

My Cousin Peggy

My cousin Peggy was born to make trouble, and it seems like every time we got together someone got a switching—usually me. One Sunday night at preaching, we were in our assigned seats when "B" walked in with a date. They sat on the left side near the back. This section was unofficially reserved for daters, but also you might see backsliders, lonely hearts, and visitors there. Peggy suggested that we move over and sit behind them so that we could monitor their actions and when we eased into the pew behind him, we got the look. However, being in church, there was nothing he could do. After a few hymns and the offering collection, I was settling in for some fire and brimstone when Peggy asked for my tie clip. Back in those days a male wore a neck tie to church, and they were generally held to your shirt with a tension loaded ornamental clip. To secure it tightly, a row of alligator teeth (serrated metal) was located on the back. She instructed me to open the clip, place it on B's ear lobe, and then let it close—which I did. Well, you would have thought we had shot him. He turned red, ripped the clip from his ear and threw it at me. Things were about to get uglier when Peggy insisted we settle down and act church appropriate. That was Peggy—instigate the trouble then wash her hands of it by acting the saintly peacemaker. About thirty years later at a relative's wedding, she came in and sat beside me; and I reminded her that I had received a whipping the last time we sat together in church. She said, "Don't worry, nobody wears tie clips anymore." Smiling devilishly she asked, "By the way, do you have any chewing gum?"

The Brahma Bull

Several weeks after Wup and I encountered the rattle snake, we were back on the trail headed for Shelter Rock once again. This time we decided to take the long way through the upper pasture to avoid going anywhere near where we encountered the snake several weeks earlier. As we crossed through the large pasture, my first inkling that something was amiss was when I felt the ground rumbling, and then I heard snorting. The bull charging toward us was not just a male cow—it was a 2,000 pound Brahma bull complete with a big white hump on top of his neck and a bad reputation. Wup was, excluding Daddy, the smartest one in the family and knew that it was her he was after. To draw the threat away from me, she ran to the other side of the field with the bull hot on her trail and in the meantime, I ran to the barbed wire fence and began to crawl under. Wup was now safe on the other side, but she continued to bark at the bovine beast until I was safe, and then she came around where I was. Nothing beats a smart dog. The only problem was that now we had to go back to the Catfish Pond and cross that dam where the rattle snake had been seen. This time I was paying attention to Wup, and at the first sign of trouble, we would be headed back home.

No Goats Allowed

Growing up on a farm was great, and one of the best things was going to the cow sale. Daddy closed his store on Tuesday afternoons and would take me to Pageland where the cattle auction was held. There you could certainly buy cows, but many other things were for sale as well and some were quite unusual—like whips, hats, belt buckles, and on and on. Once a guy was trying to sell a rifle and was about to prove its accuracy on a big black snake when another man produced a pistol and said, "If you shoot my pet snake, I'll shoot you." Thankfully no triggers were pulled. Later on that day I mentioned that I would like to have one of the many goats for sale, so Daddy bought me one. He was a "Billy Goat" and proved not to be such a good pet. That goat was mean and would butt you for no good reason. Once we found him on top of the barn eating a sweet feed sack. He had already eaten all of the feed and somehow got the sack stuck on his horns. The next Tuesday he went back to the sale, and Daddy got his five dollars back.

Too Many Shropshires

Not only was Daddy a farmer and service station owner/operator, but he was also a mailman. His rural route was about 80 miles long with 171 boxes, and as a kid I would ride with him during the summer and place mail in the box after he handed it to me. Little did I know that in just a few years I would be destroying these same boxes with bottles, chains, and rocks, but that's another story and possibly another book. Anyway it was on his mail route that Daddy and I spent real quality time together, and we developed a very strong father/son relationship. Stories of his early life in Heath Springs and from the war were passed to me during this time, and although many knew him as a war hero, I just knew that nobody was more exciting to be with. On the Walker Road we would stop and take a leak off the old wooden bridge, and occasionally he would let me shoot the sawed-off shotgun he carried for snakes. At one place we would leave corn for turkeys and at another place locus fruit for deer just in hopes of seeing them the next day. I loved spending that time with Daddy and hearing about everything he had seen and done. He had a way of making everything fun and interesting especially his stories—Pretty soon I would be a teenager and no longer listen to anybody about anything. Delivering the mail was exciting, and I was always amazed by how smart Daddy was and how he could remember who lived where and what mail went in which box. Take for example the Shopshires. They had four boxes all side by side. First there was Mr. Jimmy

Shopshire, and then just plain Jimmy Shopshire followed by Big Jimmy and of course Little Jimmy. Mr. Shopshire's wife's name was Jimmie Lee and her sister Mammy was married to just plain Jimmy. Delores was married to Big Jimmy and her best friend Margaret was Little Jimmy's wife. All of these couples had numerous little Shopshires, but Daddy always knew the correct box in which to place the mail.

Part 3

No Rock Like Shelter Rock

Shelter Rock

About two miles south of Heath Springs on Flat Rock Road, you will find an odd rock formation consisting of one large rock with another large rock precariously leaning against it and between the two rocks is a sheltering space which provided safety for the locals many years ago—thus the name Shelter Rock. Over the years Shelter Rock not only served as a local landmark, but also played an important role in history as young Andrew Jackson and his older brother Robert were there holding horses for the patriots during the Battle of Hanging Rock. It was there that Jackson was captured and taken to Camden as a prisoner of war. My father's farm lay directly across the road from Shelter Rock so when Daddy built a large lake and opened his service station there the name was a no brainer—Shelter Rock Service Station and Shelter Rock Lake. This small country store was quite the lively place during the fifties, sixties, and seventies as sooner or later everyone in the surrounding area visited. During the summer on Saturdays, it was not uncommon for the group of young men working there to wash as many as forty-five cars. Daddy was a great mentor to his employees and in the future these young men would become fine citizens and their ranks would include doctors, lawyers, bankers, and even an astronaut. Daddy's business was successful because he was a good businessman and always treated all people fairly.

That Darn Ski Belt

As a very young man, most summer days I could be found at my Daddy's store—Shelter Rock Service Station. Much of my time was spent sitting on the drink box, listening to some REAL story tellers like Paul Bowers, Heyward Reeves, Harold Haile, and Mr. Bufkin. Sometimes I would fish or play in the spillway of the large lake which was behind the store. My mother always worried that I might drown, so she used fishing line to sew a ski belt onto my cut-off blue jeans; and for the life of me, I could not become detached from it. I could unbuckle it though, so now instead of being around my waist, it was dragging around behind me. All throughout my life people have reminded me of that, and the very last time I talked with Mr. Bufkin he asked, "Is that ski belt still following you around?"

These fellas could really spin a yarn. . . .

Sam, in all his glory

Sam Finds a Home

William Braxton (Sheriff of Sumter County) brought Sam (the alligator) to Daddy in a dog box that fit on the back of a pick-up truck. There were six men plus me at the store that day, and we lifted the box from the truck and carried it out on the lake's dam about half way to the spillway. There we dumped Sam out, but he did not scurry off into the water like we thought but instead just stayed right there with his tail in the water and his head on the dam. After about five minutes of viewing him from all angles, it was determined that "Yes" he was a fine alligator and that Shelter Rock Lake would make him a great new home. As he was in no hurry to explore, someone decided to poke him with a broom to expedite his departure, however instead of leaving, he rose up and came forward making a hissing sound I never want to hear again. The top of the dam was about eight feet wide with water on one side and a steep slope on the other and three of the men decided to go east toward the station, and the other three went west toward the spillway. They all ran together like the three stooges. When all was said and done, everyone made it back to the store unscathed, however, no one saw where the gator went. Over the years Sam flourished in his new home and growing to a length of ten feet, became quite an attraction as people came from near and far to call him and see him swim from the far end of the lake to eat the cheese crackers they had thrown. The local newspapers including the Charlotte Observer did feature articles on Sam, and for several years he was the face of Heath Springs. Daddy could not have been happier.

The Great Bike Wreck of '65

After a few years, my new English bicycle had deteriorated a bit. It was held in first gear with baling wire, the fenders had disappeared, and the hand brakes were gone—no brakes at all. I was headed for Daddy's store going down C B Reeves Hill as fast as humanly possible for a 12-year-old, when it became time to apply the Flintstone Brakes. I was rubbing my right foot against the front tire when all of a sudden it lodged between the tire and frame fork. Head over heels I went, and when I stopped sliding on the tar and gravel road, I was bleeding from my chin, right elbow, and both knees. I approached the store with the front wheel in my left hand and what was left of my bicycle in my right. Daddy washed away the blood at the lake and put kerosene on my wounds. Mr. Haile said that was the worst bicycle wreck he had ever seen, and Mr. Bufkin exclaimed, "Damn boy—I have seen dead people that didn't look that bad!"

Quick Wit

Growing up at Daddy's service station, I interacted with some quick witted people. One day a fellow drove up to the pumps and quipped, "Is this gas any good?" "It must be," said Mr. Pum. "Nobody ever brought any back."

Politics Come to Shelter Rock

One day "Bad Eye" (a local political boss) stopped by the store. He told Daddy that he would like to speak with him in private. Since I was the only one there, I assumed that he didn't want me to hear—you know how that was going to work out. They went behind the counter and to shorten my story, Bad Eye wanted Daddy to run for an elected county position in hopes that he would win and thus settle an old political score of his. He had a reputation for trying to un-do, out-do, and/or who-do folks, and it turned out that his mark happened to be an old friend of Daddy's. "There's only one problem Beecher," said Bad Eye, "we know that you don't have much education, and there is some concern about your math skills. I just need for you to tell me, how good you are with math?" "Well, to answer your question," Daddy said, "as far as my math skills, nobody ever sh*# me out of any money, and as far as running against Ernest, no sawed-off worm of a politician ever talked me into betraying a friend." Bad Eye left, and I never saw him again.

"Bum" Cunningham

One day, a lady drove up to the store and asked to speak to Mr. Beecher. She told Daddy that her husband had just died. "Bum thought so much of you," she said to Daddy. "Bum" Cunningham was among the last of the few black (Lancaster County) World War I Veterans and was a fine man Daddy told us. Mrs. Cunningham agreed, and went on to say that Bum was not the same after the war. She said that when he got home, he acted differently. "He drank himself to death," she said, "he would have lived to be an old man if he had not drank and smoked so much." I asked, "How old was he?" "Ninety-two," she replied with tears in her eyes. We all looked at each other, but nobody knew what to say—not even Mr. Bufkin.

Baby Blue Eyes

One day, Mr. Hunter drove up to Daddy's store and parked his pick-up out near the lake. Soon, a group of men had gathered around the bed of the truck peering in and pointing. I knew that there was something interesting in there so I ran and jumped on the side step and leaned in—almost landing in the bed. There on a board, stretched out straight, was a monstrous rattlesnake. He must have been six feet long and as big around as your leg. His mouth was held open with a stick, exposing the fangs which were longer than my fingers, but worst of all were his eyes—they were baby blue. I will never forget those eyes for as long as I live. Seeing this sight made playing in the woods less appealing.

Play Ball

Many notable people visited Daddy's store. One day a well-dressed man came in for a coke and pack of crackers. He was about to leave when I recognized him from the crusade/revival I had attended in Lancaster the week before. "Aren't you B---- R---------?" I asked. As soon as he acknowledged that he was, several of the men gathered around and began talking to him. I just stood back and listened, but before he left he walked over to me and asked if I was a baseball fan. We talked about several teams and players—batting averages and other statistics. Sometimes you just know when somebody is special, and that was certainly the feeling I got after talking to Bobby Richardson.

Where Policy Is Made

If you have ever flown in or out of Washington, DC, more than likely you passed through Dulles International Airport. John Foster Dulles was a well-known national statesman during the forties and fifties serving as Secretary of State for Dwight Eisenhower. He was also friends with US Congressman J P Richards, who lived just down the road from us—Daddy would look after Mr. Richards' cows when he was in Washington. One afternoon in 1951, Mr. Dulles and Congressman Richards spent the afternoon at the store discussing the issues of the day. Fighting the spread of Communism and establishing the Interstate Highway System were hot topics at that time, and I would not be surprised if Mr. Dulles acquired some new policy ideas before leaving Shelter Rock. If nothing else, he had been exposed to the Deep South and some of its characters, and that would be a good thing for anybody.

Number 11

One day, a flatbed truck carrying a race car stopped at the store and out stepped Ned Jarrett. I was already inspecting the car when Ned told me to climb up and get in if I wanted to—He was a very nice man. Never will I forget sitting in that car and acting as if I was driving in a race. The steering wheel was huge and wrapped neatly with black electrical tape, but everything else seemed junky— wires and half connected parts everywhere. It smelled like grease. Nevertheless it made a memorable impression on me, and I could say that I drove "The Champ's" blue number 11—even if it was only pretend.

Supreme Commander

Shelter Rock Lake is teeming with life especially in the upper end where the water is shallow. On summer nights the sounds are almost deafening with creatures large and small, looking for love or maybe just singing for the pleasure of it. One night I walked onto what we referred to as the island, (a narrow strip of land extending out into the lake for about 50 feet) in the midst of the night noises and shouted to the top of my capacity—SHUT UP! There was total silence, I mean total silence for about five seconds then one brave soul croaked then another, and soon all of the multitudes were at it again. But for a brief few seconds, they were all silent. Talk about feeling powerful.

Low Riding Cadillac

One Saturday afternoon, a Cadillac pulled up to the pumps for some gas. I noticed that the car was riding very low to the ground and when I saw who was inside, it was evident why. Driving the Caddy was Two-Ton Harris and his passengers were Haystack Calhoun, Swede Hanson, Brute Bernard, and Skull Murphy. (For you youngsters, these men were the stars of professional wrestling in the sixties). They were bound for Sumter and seemed a little perturbed that we had no alcohol for sale. Judging by the amount of empty beer cans, they didn't need any more. Even if they weren't the friendliest customers we ever had, they paid with a fifty-dollar bill, so at least I was impressed with that. Anyway, I thought it odd that they would ride together seeing how they hated each other so much, but I decided not to mention it because they were in a hurry.

Part 4

Oh, the Things We Did

Ghost of Hanging Rock

One day when I was about 14 years old, Wup and I were hunting squirrels in the woods behind Daddy's service station. It was a very damp day, and occasionally light showers would occur at which time we would seek shelter beside one of the many large rocks that dotted the hillside. Crouching down and becoming as small as possible was the best way to stay dry. As the shower was ending and I was beginning to stand, I felt a hand on my shoulder. Attempting to turn around, I found that I could not—something was holding me, and for about five seconds I could not move as whatever it was maintained a grip on me. Finally I broke free by swinging my elbows violently, but falling to the ground in the process. Upon standing, I began looking around trying to determine what had just happened to me when I heard a strange noise as if someone was moaning. Wup had been acting strangely throughout the entire event, and it was she who decided that it was time to go—we ran almost all the way back home. The Battle of Hanging Rock occurred on this exact location in 1780 with the American Patriots defeating the British in a very bloody encounter. Two hundred British soldiers and twenty-two Americans were killed there on that hillside, and I will always believe that somehow one of them encountered me that day.

The Perfect Partnership

Back in the '60s, there was one farmer in town that personified how government and a private business could work together. Mr. Bowers' elder son drove a school bus. During the weekend, Mr. Bowers would modify the bus by removing the seats and disconnecting the speedometer cable, thus creating the perfect vehicle for hauling hay from the field to the barn. After the work was complete, a good hosing out would remove any residual Bermuda grass and give the appearance that above average care was taken of the bus. Reinstall the seats, reconnect the cable, and add a little replacement gas and *voilà!* There you have a private business working hand-in-hand with the government, even if the government didn't know about it.

Reel to Reel

Mr. Reeves worked for the Heath Springs Light and
Power Company, and his son "Buzz" was a good friend of
mine. Occasionally, Mr. Reeves would acquire a reel or
spool on which telephone wire came from the factory. The
reel stood about six feet tall and had a small compart-
ment in the middle just big enough for a small person to
enter. There was a metal bar extending through the middle so if you were fool enough to ride; you could at least
brace yourself by holding onto it. One day, George, Dru,
Ricky, Buzz, and I decided to take turns riding the reel
down the hill nearby. This proved to be a bad idea because
first of all, there was no way to stop and second, you could
get killed. Nevertheless, we took turns riding and enjoying the drunkenness which followed. Talk about fun, we
were having it until George was stung by a wasp. Risking
our lives riding down the hill was acceptable, however, a
wasp sting really hurt.

Chevelle Versus Train

OK friends, here's one for the ages. In the late sixties, some teenagers in the area were known to position their car on the railroad tracks so that you could ride the rails. Many miles had been logged on the tracks, and several trestles in the area had been successfully crossed, however, no one had attempted the big one—the one over the Catawba River near the Bowater Paper Mill. One summer night, four teenagers from Heath Springs were on the tracks and approaching this trestle bridge when a dim light appeared in the distance. As the light grew larger and the realization of what was about to happen became evident, panic set in and the car became wedged in the tracks. The boys abandoned the vehicle and from the safety of an oak grove witnessed a sight that few can only imagine. It was said the Sea Board Coastline freight train was traveling almost 40 mph when it struck the car, catapulting it 10 feet into the air and causing it to look as if it had been, well—hit by a train. A thorough investigating revealed no injuries were sustained and no major damage to the train occurred, however, some track repair would be necessary. By now the sun was rising over the Catawba River and the boys had made good use of the night to work out their story, but no amount of time would be sufficient. Jimmy did the best he could, however, when he told the investigating officer and I quote—"We were looking for a shortcut to highway number 9."

Cornbread Dressing

When Lynda my future sister-in-law's parents came to Heath Springs to meet the Hortons for the first time, Mama had warned me that if I did or said anything which in any way could be considered crude, unkind, or distasteful that she would beat me within inches of my life. The Reids were very nice and very proper and, although "B" was due in the payback department, I had no preconceived notion to ruin his future by making an uncouth statement or inappropriate gesture. However, upon my first bite of the dressing which Mrs. Reid had prepared, I said, "Eew, Mama, what's wrong with this dressing?" For the next few seconds, time seemed to stand still and everything was in slow motion. Mama was beet red, with steam coming from her ears. Something bad was surely about to happen to me; however, just in the nick of time Mrs. Reid rescued me. She said, "That's OK, Mac. Nobody's cooking tastes as good as Mama's cooking." She had taken me off the hook, for which I was forever grateful. By the way, B and Lynda did get married and still are.

Love at First Sight

When I was in the ninth grade, Daddy reminded me that soon I would want a car, which meant that I was going to need to start saving money. His idea was for me to raise several calves on a bucket so that in a year or so, they would be ready for sale. I did, and sure enough by the time I entered the eleventh grade, I had $500.00; therefore, my search for the ultimate ride was on. While checking out car lots in Lancaster, something near the back of the property caught my eye. Upon further inspection, it turned out to be a 1966 Mustang that had just come in—not even yet ready for sale. It was a 289 navy blue convertible with a white top and white interior. Without even driving it, I knew that car was for me. My problem was the price, as the salesman was firm at $800. "Just look at it, Daddy," I said. He did and, just like me, he knew it had "Mac" written all over it. He gave me the three hundred dollars needed to complete the transaction, and I entered teenage heaven. As it turned out, that Mustang was probably the best vehicle I ever owned. I drove it two years in high school plus four years while in college, and I drove it hard. Upon attaining my degree, my first educated decision was to sell my 1966 Mustang convertible and buy an MGB. So much for higher learning.

The Spit Wad

In the ninth grade, some of the boys in our class went through a spitball shooting phase. It was not uncommon to see someone nailed from across the room with a shot blown through a drinking straw; however, pretty soon this became boring, so now it became time to move up to the next level in spitball-ology. Benny was just the man to develop the super spit wad. He would place an entire sheet of paper in his mouth until it became sloppy—with the consistency of paste. At this time, he would spit the wad in his hand and throw it straight up to the ceiling. Spreading out to about the size of a dinner plate, it would stick there on the tile. About five years after the school closed, I went into that old classroom and was moved by the memories of so many good times and funny experiences that had occurred there. Gazing around the room, my eyes eventually reached the ceiling, and Benny's super spit wad was still there.

Betrayed

On our way home from school one day, Dru, Mike, and I began horsing around. Traveling about 55 mph, Mike threw one of my books out of the window—my papers, homework, etc. was scattered all along the roadside. Looking around for one of Mike's books, I was about to get even when Dru handed me a book and said, "Throw Mike's book out." I immediately slung it as hard and as far as I could. My best friend in the world had handed me one of my own books. They got a good laugh at my expense, but I have a long memory and pay back is coming when they least expect it.

Only the Brave

Going through the Brewer cabin late at night was not for the faint of heart. Dr. Brewer owned a large estate which consisted of the house (Brewer Mansion) and a cabin located about a mile from the mansion, way back in the woods. All of this was in disrepair by the late sixties and perfect for scaring the wits out of teenagers late at night. Digging the well for the mansion, two men died when striking a pocket of methane gas, so there was already the potential for ghosts in the area. The cabin was on a hillside accessible only by crossing the dam of a large lake which lay in front of the cabin and at night a low dense fog always hovered over the water. A large rock (about 10 feet tall) with a flat top served as the front porch, and it had steps going up both sides to the top of the rock and from there you would enter the cabin. One night, Jimmy, Reggie, and I decided to explore this ghostly structure. We parked the car on Twitty Mill Road and walked about two miles down a trail arriving at the lake's dam. We stood there looking upwards toward the house pondering our next decision, and by the light of the moon and two small flashlights, we went in. It was very dark, but it appeared to be one big room with stairs leading to a lower floor. I did not see a back door, and trust me, I was looking for one. The walls were covered with graffiti, and in the middle of the floor lay a tarp dotted with red spots—it could have been blood. All of a sudden Reggie dropped his light and yelled something. We all took off. People thought

Jimmy was fast—well, I was back on the dam before Jimmy got to the bottom of the steps. We decided not to go back for the flashlight, and as a matter of fact, I never went back.

Three Licks or Three Days

P E (physical education) was mandatory for all ninth graders, and we were engrossed in tumbling. I persuaded Mike and Ricky to help me move the basketball scorer's table from the bleachers to the gym floor so we could use it as a prop to tumble over; however, as we returned the table to its rightful position, it was dropped and after doing a little tumbling its self—was broken. We did the best we could to repair it and then slipped out the back door. Later that day we found ourselves in Mr. Brown's office being grilled. My position was that Yes, I was there; however, I never touched the table (which was a lie), but I had heard about high school punishment and was determined to avoid a paddling at any cost. Mike and Ricky were found innocent, but my option was three licks or three days—I opted for the three days. I told Mama that I did not break the table and was hoping to just leave it there and enjoy my mini vacation, however, Mama was determined that her son would not be falsely accused or punished for something he did not do. One thing about Mama—she would stand up for her children (especially me), and no one or no thing on this earth would dissuade her if she believed that one of hers was being treated unfairly. The next day I went to school, and Mrs. Horton went to see Mr. Brown. As it turns out Mr. Brown, as tough as he was, was no match for Mary Horton when defending her son and although everybody on God's green earth knew I was guilty, she felt otherwise. Honestly I never felt right about the whole thing because after all I did break the table, and then told two lies. My web of deceit was weighing heavy on my conscious, and I really could have used those three days to pull myself back together.

Dashing Through the Snow

One winter when I was about sixteen years old, we had an accumulation of snow amounting to about three inches. That night we used a ski rope to tie a sled to the rear of the '53 Ford I was driving at the time and several of us were having the time of our lives on one of the dirt roads in Pleasant Hill. It was so dark that we (in the car) could not see Mike on the sled so the plan was that if, for any reason, he wanted me to slow down or stop, he would turn on his flashlight as a signal. When we got to the end of the road and began the turn around process, there was no Mike and only an upside down sled. As I drove back, we met Mike walking, and he was bleeding profusely from a cut on his face. He explained that he tried to hold on, but the last curve was too sharp and I was going too fast, thus dragging him through the ditch. "You should have turned on your flashlight," I said, to which he replied, "I DID." Sure enough, after we drove back to the curve, we found his flashlight lying in the middle of the road. It was on.

The Old Richards House

About one mile from where we lived stood the old Richards house. It was the crème of ghost houses; and I spent one night there in the sixties, but before I tell the tale, let me share some background. The house was built in the early 1800s in the antebellum style—three story, huge porches with columns, and white. There were many large oak trees in the yard surrounding the house. Legend has it that General Sherman stayed the night; however, he slept in a tent preferring to have the same accommodations as his men. There were other legends—some a bit less admirable. Like the time when a friendly poker game took a turn that resulted in an ax murder, or the tale about a young slave girl that was buried alive underneath the house. If there was such a thing as ghosts, this would be the perfect place for one to reside. By the mid-sixties, Mr. Stitzel had purchased the home and lived there with his elderly mother. From time to time his work would require him to be out of town overnight, and on one such occasion he asked me to spend the night and look after things. I agreed because ten dollars was ten dollars, and Daddy said that it might be an adventure—was he ever right. I arrived late and watched TV until it signed off. Then I retired to my room which was at the top of the stairs on the left. Lutzi, (German for Lucy) the big German shepherd house dog who befriended me and on whom I depended for protection, laid at the top of the stairs. There was no A/C in the house and all I had for cover was a sheet. Almost as soon as I went to bed, I heard a thump at the bottom of the stairs—then another and another. Something was coming up the stairs. Lutzi began to bark and continued barking furiously while simultaneously backing into my room—now she was growling and was all the way back to my bed. I was terrified beyond description and under the sheet I went because if I was going to be ax murdered or strangled by the spirit of that slave girl, I didn't want to see it. Then Lutzi darted from the room and stopped half way down the stairs—still barking. I lay there sweating—I lay there sweating all night and by morning the entire bed was soaked. There is no doubt in my mind that someone/something came in my room that night; and whatever it was, was deterred by Lutzi. At the crack of dawn I was out of there with my ten dollars and my adventure.

How to Make Daddy Cuss

The driveway to Dru's house was shaped like a horseshoe. You could enter one side, drive to the back, then exit by going on around and out the other side. The summer of 1969 had been very eventful and resulted with several of us being in trouble regarding some damaged mailboxes. We needed to talk things over so to see Dru, I went. As I proceeded up the driveway and around the house, in the back yard was a police car; and through the large back bay window I could see Dru, his Daddy, and a policeman talking. I could see them looking and pointing at me as I eased by, so I just gave a little wave and scooted on around. I did not go home but returned later to pick up Dru and his brother John so we could further discuss our predicament. We wound up riding on a sandy dirt road going just fast enough to slide a little while weaving from ditch to ditch. Then I went a little too far and lost it. We jumped the ditch and blazed a path through a stand of pine trees, coming to rest precariously on a large pine that was not all the way down. Our first thought was to sweep the road with some of the available pine tops to conceal the evidence, but that made it worse—much worse. John's wrist was cracked and hurting so we decided it was time to fess up. Dru's father took me home to face the music. Upon returning to the crash site with my Daddy, evidence of what had taken place was all around us and upon seeing his '53 Ford balanced precariously on a leaning pine, was livid. "God Almighty Damn, son—your driving days are over!" he said. And Daddy never cussed.

Too Cool for School

One of the funniest events of my life has to do with typing class. At Heath Springs High School, the typing room was located in Mrs. Steele's homeroom—separated by a glass wall. Mitchell was so unruly that she made him sit, by himself, in the typing room so she could call the roll without interruption. Mitchell moved the carriage of the typewriter so that when she called his name all he had to do was hit the space bar and "DING." I can still see the grin on his face. Maybe you had to be there, but I had to visit Mr. Brown because I couldn't stop laughing.

Mission Impossible

As the school year of 1969 neared its end and exam time loomed large, it became evident that Mrs. Lindler's biology exam would make or break several of our classmates who were in grave danger of failing the tenth grade. The test consisted of thirty multiple choice and twenty true/false questions and was renowned for its difficulty and feared by all who teetered near the pass/fail line. Something had to be done to rescue our classmates so a plan was devised and set in motion. Operation "Everyone Passes" was dependent on Donna's ability to leave the last window in the Home Economics classroom unlocked, and she came through in flying colors as the window was not only unlocked, but also cracked about an inch. Slithering through the opening, three young men gained entry to the school and made their way directly to the biology lab where in Mrs. Lindler's desk drawer they found and pilfered a copy of the multiple choice section of the exam—in and out in less than ten minutes. The correct answers were later determined and distributed to all who desired them. Phase two involved implementation of our true/false solution. As the questions were read, Ricky would indicate the correct answer by the position of his pencil. If he held the eraser end up, the answer was true, and if he held the pointed end up then the answer was false. In the past she had always read the true/false questions to us, however, on the day of the exam she announced a change and indicated that these questions would not be read aloud. "But Mrs. Lindler," Donna said, "I think we all do better when you read the statement." There was a collective nodding of heads and "yes" was mumbled by everyone and so she relented. No one had ever scored 100 on the tenth grade biology exam, but with a little help from some friends, seven people had a perfect score that day and the lowest grade in the class was 88. Everyone became a junior.

High Times

Once upon a time a long time ago, a car load of young people was traveling from Myrtle Beach to Cherry Grove. Back then, that stretch of Highway 17 was void of commercialization and was almost like a country road. The highway patrolman who stopped them asked the driver if he knew why he was being pulled over. When Tommy answered, "No Sir," the officer said, "son you've been driving 16 mph for the last four miles, and I thought something might be wrong. Can I see your driver's license?" Looking at the license (which included address) the patrolman asked, "Tommy, do you live in Kershaw?" Tommy looked up at him with the widest triumphant grin and said, "You know me maaaaaan? How do you know me man?" You can figure out the rest.

Hold On to Your Hat

In 1970 our three small schools in Lancaster County consolidated to form Andrew Jackson High School. Although in the past Flat Creek, Heath Springs, and Kershaw had been bitter rivals, this was a new day, and we were very excited regarding the many possibilities that awaited us. Football was the life blood of the community, and there were high expectations from the team. With a well endowed booster club, the players were treated like royalty as we wore monogram orange blazers, orange and white shirts, ate hamburger steaks together, and rode to non-home games on a chartered bus. The Monday after our first away game, the football team was called to a meeting. Mr. Brown came in, slammed the door, walked to the front of the room and glared at us for about 30 seconds. Finally he said, "I don't know who stole that bus driver's cap, but if it is not in my office within 24 hours some of you in this room are going to be mighty sorry." Even though most guys on the team barely knew each other, no one ratted out the culprits; and Mr. Brown never found the cap. The caper remains (officially) unsolved to this day.

Larry Meets Leon

Leon was a running back for York High School in the early seventies, and he was very good. Standing about six feet two inches, he was a man among boys. We lost that game, and Coach Neal was very upset so Monday was a rough day at practice. Tuesday was film day, and we were all watching as we relived the initial kick off. Leon received the ball and as he proceeded up the right sideline, flat ran over someone. "Stop the film!" Coach Neal shouted. "Who is that arm tackling—You can't bring down a man like that by arm tackling. Who is that?" It was Larry. The Coach berated Larry, recalling every missed tackle in the history of football, and reminding him that any further arm tackling would be punishable by extended practice time. He said that if he ever again saw any arm tackling by anyone on the team, we all would be running wind sprints until Thursday. "OK, restart the film," he said. Leon continued down the sideline until surrounded, at which time he switched direction and proceeded across the field towards the left sideline. WHAM! He ran over another one of our players, and Coach Neal nearly came out of his shoes. "Arm tackling—Arm tackling!" he shouted. "This is why we lost this game. Stop the film—Who is it this time?" It was Larry again. Leon had run over Larry twice on the same play. Although Larry was having a bad night, my helmet was off to him. At least he slowed Leon down.

Dude, Where's My Car?

In the early seventies, multi-day outdoor concerts were the rage. Rockingham Motor Speedway was holding an event billed as Woodstock South, hosting bands such as the Allman Brothers, Marshall Tucker, Three Dog Night, Rod Stewart, and the like. We were going, and Terry was driving his Volvo. Arriving on Saturday about noon, we settled in one of four large fields designated for camping and parking. The event really was similar to Woodstock, complete with huge quantities of drugs, real hippies, and even a thunderstorm. Partying hard until Sunday afternoon, it was finally time to head for home—all we had to do was find the car. Searching the field where we thought it was proved fruitless, so we walked to the other parking areas, coming up empty, as well. The hunt went on all afternoon and by now the other cars were gone—all that remained were several tents sporadically dotted over the vacated fields. As darkness began to descend, worry set in; and by now only one large campsite was left. Upon further inspection, we found that the party goers next to our car had covered two cars with a huge canvas making their nest; and yes, our car was under the canvas. "Dude, we've been looking for this car for hours. Didn't it cross your mind that we might need to go home?" I asked. "Sorry man," he replied, "we thought everyone was staying until Sunday." Reminding him that it WAS Sunday would have served no useful purpose.

Piss Road

Piss Road is a legendary three quarter mile straight stretch of asphalt situated about two miles from downtown Kershaw. It's where all unsanctioned events in the Heath Springs/Kershaw area take place. Fights, drag races, and of course relieving yourself, would be common occurrences. One night the word around town was, there was going to be a girl fight on Piss Road at nine o'clock. The principals (we were told) were from Bone Town, which had a reputation for producing tough customers and good fighters. When we got there at 8:45, there were already about twenty cars lining both sides of the road, and sure enough at the appointed time, two girls emerged and immediately began fighting. This was no dainty affair, as there was plenty of cussing, hair pulling, and ripping of clothing. The larger girl was clearly winning so, after about five minutes, some other girls stepped in and stopped it. We all agreed that it was a good fight and then resumed riding around—just another Saturday night in Ktown.

Out in Right Field

One summer night, Rusty and I were riding around in Heath Springs. As we drove down Roland Avenue by the baseball field, Rusty decided that it would be a good idea to circle the bases in his car. So after touching home plate down the first base line we went, as fast as a 1950 Ford would go. Our turn was a little wide, and we wound up in right field, stuck up to the axle. We tried rocking, pushing, and praying; but it was only getting worse. I noticed a round light on my leg, and soon Mr. Ballard, our town policeman, came walking out of the spotlight. "I'm afraid to ask," he said, "but what are you boys doing out here?" My answer was outstanding, second only to Jimmy's—"looking for a short cut to highway number 9" (you remember the car on the trestle incident). I said, "There is a game tomorrow, and we were checking out the condition of the field." Mr. Ballard said, "Well, I haven't heard that one before, but I haven't seen a Ford stuck in the outfield before either." After helping us get out he said, "Boys, let's just keep this between us." I always liked him.

Hurry Sundown

Sunrise Lake was a well known "Lovers' Lane" in the Heath Springs area by dating couples, young and old. You could park on a grassy area and enjoy a view of the lake or you could venture to a more private section located up near the trees. On Saturday night it could get a little crowded so arriving early was recommended. Dru and I were double dating two young ladies from Kershaw and after some small talk decided to mosey on over to the lake. When we got there it was still daylight, and once again we had fallen victim to poor planning. Since there is nothing more awkward than lovers' lane during the day, we rode around—and around and around. Finally darkness befell the land so back to the lake we drove. Now we could get down to some serious smooching in the privacy of night time, if we could find a parking place.

Walk a Mile in My Shoes

Jimmy and I had been on several long walk abouts, and one day we decided to walk from Heath Springs to Camden and back by way of Flat Rock Road—about 50 miles round trip. In preparation, the previous day we strategically placed jars of water along the way so we would not have to carry it—pretty smart, right? At 4 am on Sunday morning, we departed from the caution light in Heath Springs, and by the time the sun rose, we were about a fourth of the way there. We had a great adventure walking and talking and by noon, we were at the Camden town limits sign. Resting in the woods, we ate the lunch that we had brought and carved a "J" on a large oak tree, as both our names were James. Still feeling pretty good, we started back. Instead of returning the same way we had come, for some reason we decided to go back through Kershaw, which added about 15 extra miles—no problem. About four o'clock, it was becoming a big problem. We were miles from Kershaw, and I was worn out. The huge mistake we made was stopping for a coke at one of the country stores, as standing up after sitting down was brutal. We had walked about another three miles when a friend came checking on us—we were still about 3 miles from Kershaw. At first Jimmy insisted that we not accept the ride, but we were both done. The next day my legs were sore, and I was unable to go to school—at least I got a day off out of it.

Hooked on Fishing

One Saturday night we had a party at the Horton river cabin. Everyone was there, and I must say it was quite an event. The gathering began to thin out near the wee hours, and only the hard core partiers remained—about four guys. Howard recommended that we go fishing as, according to him, he knows where they are and how to catch them. Back to Kershaw we drove to collect the proper paraphernalia then we were off towards Camden. Turning from the main road onto a dirt road, we continued to travel until, finally, we were on a pulpwood road. We were in a jeep so rocks and small trees presented no problem as we proceeded further and further back into the woods. Eventually, we came to a clearing within sight of the rock filled river. So many rocks, in fact, I said to myself that this is a wasted trip because no fish of any size could live here. As they headed down to the river bank, I decided to take a nap in the jeep, believing that no fish would be caught this morning. In about forty-five minutes, they returned with eight striped bass weighting approximately ten pounds apiece. That was when I learned something about fishing—some people do it haphazardly to relax, but some people take it seriously and know what they are doing.

Take No Prisoners

During the summers of my youth, I worked at Springs Park. It was the best job imaginable, and I still can't believe they paid me. There were plenty of girls in bikinis and an Olympic-sized swimming pool with a four-tiered 10 meter diving platform. That's over thirty feet folks, and yes I did—we all did. One day the filter for the pool became clogged so the boss sent Jerry, Chucky, and me to Chester in a big flatbed truck to get a load of sand which was necessary to implement the repair. During the drive, Jerry figured out how to make the truck backfire, and he did not discriminate among his victims. Man-woman, black-white, young or old, if you were within 100 feet of the road you got the bang. He fired on a woman sitting on her porch and on a man riding a horse. I tried to deter him as we approached an older lady walking with a young girl; however, it was to no avail. I don't think I have ever laughed so hard in my life. You would not believe the motions people make with their arms/hands when they think they have been shot.

Part 5

Sir, Yes Sir

Decisions, Decisions

At the Citadel, choosing a major course of study for your college experience is an important decision and should be decided upon with much thought and consideration. I had pre-registered as a Political Science Major, but when the actual sign-up time arrived, I found myself in line behind six other guys. My shoes and brass needed shining and polishing and right beside me was the Psychology Station with no line at all. Everyone takes the same thing for the first two years anyway, and since I was in a hurry. . . . I stepped up, and Colonel Bowman asked, "Why do you want to major in Psychology?" I said, "I have always been intrigued by the effects of environment on one's personality and have often wondered which plays the greater role in personality development—heredity or environment." He said, "That sounds like bullshit. . . . You'll be perfect. Sign here."

Not my most relaxed moment in life.

Hell Night

At the Citadel, there is a thing called "Hell Night." They bring all of the freshmen out onto the quad and turn off all the lights—you could hear a pin drop. After a couple of minutes of terrifying silence, the gate is slammed shut and the announcement is made that the fourth class system is now in effect. Upper classmen come running at you from everywhere yelling, screaming, and soaking you with buckets of water. You are running in place, holding your rifle over your head, then doing push-ups, and more running in place. This goes on for quite a while, and at some point during the confusion, an upper classman (with a shaven head) slips into our ranks. All of a sudden this guy takes off running for the gate shouting, "I can't take it anymore!" One of the upper classmen produces a starter's pistol and fires at him. He slides to a stop on the wet quad and is laying there motionless—looking dead to me. "Get back to your rooms and keep your mouths shut," screams the first sergeant. WELL. . . . I thought to myself—this will surely be in the paper.

It Could Have Been a Lot Worse

For knobs at the Citadel venturing outside of your room could have disastrous consequences, but there was a drink machine on the first floor; and if one wanted a coke bad enough, some chances would have to be taken. One night Kim and I were in desperate need of some caffeine, so I told him that I would fly if he would buy. I made it all the way to the sally port unscathed, however, waiting there were all twelve members of the 1973 Junior Sword Drill. For those of you not familiar with Citadel customs and traditions, I will just say that for a freshman to run into this group is not a good thing. I determined that my best choice of poison was just to keep running, and although this would land me in dreaded "G" Company, nothing could be worse than where I was. As I tried to scoot on by, my First Sergeant recognized me and ordered me to halt. "Well Horton," he said, "looks like this is your lucky night." I realized that nothing good could possibly come from this and had accepted the fact that there were many push-ups in my immediate future. Then one of them said that if I would answer one question honestly I could go. "Which one of us is the ugliest?" he asked. Now I felt a little better as they were all ugly and at least I could make eleven of them happy. "He is," I said, "pointing to a short fellow in the back." My answer was met with overwhelming agreement and before any retaliation could occur I was told to get back to my room. When Kim asked where the cokes were, I told him what had happened and how narrow my escape had been—we decided to swear off soft drinks for a while as they could be hazardous to your health.

Have You Seen Junior's Grades?

If your child's grades aren't very good after one half se-
mester in college, don't worry—all may not be lost. At
mid-semester my freshman year, I had one A, one C,
three Ds and one F. My roommate was sporting five Fs
and a D in Air Force. We managed to improve somewhat
and by Christmas were both passing almost everything.
I maintained my A in English by getting one question
right. One day, we were excruciatingly dissecting a poem,
when Major Alexander called on me to answer why the
tent (in the poem) was supported by a cedar post. I answered, "Because cedar won't rot." He grabbed his chest,
took a few steps backward and said, "I've been teaching
this course two times a day for twenty years, and nobody
ever correctly answered that question until now." Daddy
told me that learning to repair barbed wire fences would
come in handy one day, and he was right—again.

Musical Gizzards

My freshman year I could endure the sweat parties, marathon runs, and shirt tuck events; but what I dreaded most was meal time. There were many reasons for a freshman to dislike the mess hall, and for me the worst was a game called "musical gizzards." An upper classman would close his eyes and hum a song while the four freshmen seated at each table would pass between themselves a huge plate of chicken gizzards. When he stopped humming, whoever held the plate had to eat a gizzard. They were deep fried and about the size of a fifty cent piece and so greasy they would slide right out of your hand. My First Sergeant was equal in his cruelty; and if you didn't win a gizzard, he would make you eat two at a time. I can hear him now asking the lady for additional gizzards. "My boys look extra hungry tonight," he would say.

Colonel Sominex

During freshman year at the Citadel, sleep is a precious commodity; and, if you fell asleep in class most professors would just let it go as long as you didn't disturb the others. Enter Billy, the pride of Johnsonville. He was snoring so strongly that the light passing through the window was bending and the professor had no choice but to instruct our classmate, Gary, to wake Billy. So Gary pulled his arm, and Billy's chin hit the desk—almost landing him on the floor. There was a thunderous laugh, and the professor even asked Billy if he was OK. Once we got back to our room (freshman cannot talk on campus), I asked my roommate, Bill, if he had ever seen anything so funny. Bill asked, "What are you talking about?" I said, "When Billy almost fell in the floor." Bill asked, "When?" He had slept through the whole thing.

Sorry Fokkers

I had the best college roommate. He was so witty, and NOBODY told a tale like Bill Myrick. I had mentioned in an earlier story that at mid-semester freshman year his grades were not stellar, but he was passing Air Force with a strong D. Once in class while discussing airplanes, our instructor was comparing the German Fokker to the British Spitfire. He went on and on about how the Fokker was deficient. He pointed out that it was slow to climb and turn, and even how the fuel tanks were too small. At the end of the class, he asked Bill what he had learned about this German aircraft. Bill replied, "All I know is that those Germans sure built some sorry Fokkers." Only Bill would have thought of that.

Where No Man Has Gone Before

At the Citadel, the term elective course is a misnomer—
you get a VERY narrow choice depending on your major.
My junior year, I had to take a physical science; and my
decision was between either physics or astronomy. The
mere word 'physics' frightened me so astronomy seemed
the logical choice. Besides I already knew a lot about
space, being one of the original "trekkies." Warp speed,
photon torpedo, and transporter were terms familiar to
me; and heck, I could practically speak Vulcan. Imagine
my surprise, after about a week of seeing mathematical
equations so long and complicated that it took two chalk-
boards just to compose the question—lord only knows
what the answer would take. Fortunately I was not the
only one "Lost in Space," and since Major Brown graded
strictly on the Bell Curve, somehow I wound up making
a C. Honestly, I never understood one thing that man was
talking about except when he called the role.

Peeping Cadets

One good thing about taking Astronomy was the field exercise—We called it "star gazing." We would take three small telescopes out onto one of the open fields at night and try to locate particular stars, planets, etc. Someone would distract Major Brown by saying something about a comet, (every astronomer wants to discover a new comet), and while he was seriously searching the sky, we would train the other two telescopes on the apartment complex across the way. Hey, we were young men.

Messing with the Major

I had to take Botany as one of my science courses under Major Crosby who was a good instructor but never very personable. Daddy was always up to something and once planted, in his garden, a row of pumpkins next to a row of gourds. The product resembled a giant pear. He suggested I take this Major one in an effort to break the ice and try to establish some kind of relationship. The Major could not believe his eyes as I reminded him that my family farmed and was good at it. "This is the average size of a Heath Springs Pear," I told him. He wanted to know more about it; but I hinted that you are the Botanist and that you should be able to determine the species, origin, etc. He never did and I did not enlighten him until after the grades came out—another B for me. Daddy was so smart!

How to Get Ahead in Zoology

I was not fond of any subject remotely related to Biology and often remarked that the inside of that building smelled like a D. I did, however, take Zoology where we were required to study the insides of a fetal pig and be able to identify the organs. To test our knowledge, the professor would stick small pins with different colored heads into the different organs, and students would have to identify the organ by the color of pin protruding from it. At the Citadel, things are super competitive, and it was not beyond some cadets to switch pins after recording their answers so that the next group would, even if they got it right—get it wrong. The Blue Book was clear about lying, cheating or stealing; but there was nothing prohibiting the switching of colored pins in the organs of fetal pigs.

Dine and Dash

During the summer of 1974, Jack, Gary, and I were living in an unfurnished apartment on John's Island and attending summer school. My senior year was coming up and not wanting to overburden myself during my last two semesters, I decided to knock out French 202 and an elective—Public Speaking. When I say that our apartment was unfurnished, I mean unfurnished as we had nothing, not even a TV, and on the occasion of visitors, our entertainment was tossing cards at an empty pot which sat in the corner of the living room. Gary's girlfriend, Jenny, worked as a cashier at the Trawler, one of Charleston's finer seafood restaurants, and it was she who suggested that we could eat there and not pay—Dine and Dash. This sounded like a challenge so the next Thursday night three clean cut young gentlemen entered the establishment, and proceeded to order three seafood platters. We determined that going first class would attract less attention so we acted as if fine dining was something we did all the time and what did it matter since we didn't plan to pay anyway. After our meal we strolled into the gift shop, handed Jenny our tickets, and ambled right out the door. There was no dashing at all until we got to the car at which time we tore out of the parking lot. Jenny said that it was a clean get away, and that management never suspected a thing.

Swamp People

My roommate Bill lived in Allendale which is well known for swamps and poor education. Once on an overnight from the Citadel, I went to his home for some rest and relaxation. He had arranged a blind date for me so we did the town and after returning the girls home safely wound up at the local hang-out. Mickey (one of the local good ole boys) suggested that we go to his cabin, get the boats, and check the alligator lines—which by the way was illegal at this time. So Bill, Mickey, Ralph, and I set out for the swamp in hopes of catching a gator. Bill and I were in one boat with the rifle, lantern, and paddles while Mickey and Ralph manned the second boat. After checking several lines with no success, we headed across an open area arriving at the next line. I grabbed the limb to steady myself shaking it just enough to free the cottonmouth water moccasin that was waiting there, and into the boat he fell. Bill whacked him with the paddle, but at the same time knocked the lantern into the water. We were yelling for Mickey and Ralph to come with a light because Bill and I were in one end of the boat, and a mad cottonmouth was in the other end. They arrived and Ralph extricated the monster with his frog gig. That was enough excitement for me, and I was ready to go home; however, there was one more line to check, and yes it held a gator. He was a small one weighing only about 100 pounds. After shooting him with the rifle, we loaded him up and returned to the cabin where we had a few beers and reveled in our trimphful hunt. I told them how much fun I had, and that I would surely not miss the next opportunity to cruise the swamps with them. They assured me that the next time I would be welcome. I have done some dumb things in my life, but I promise you that I will never again get into a small boat at night and paddle deep into the swamp in hopes of bagging a fierce reptile. Did I mention that the area was known for poor education?

Part 6

Live and Learn

Country Comes to Town

One day Daddy told me about his first trip to New York City. He and two friends (Kenneth and Charlie) drove from Heath Springs in his 1938 Chevy (the same one that also could thrash peas) and landed in the middle of Manhattan. Upon arriving they discovered that the pace of life was a little faster, and with no driving experience in a large city, a little intimidating. It wasn't long before they found themselves on a one way street going the wrong way. "I didn't know there were that many car horns in the world," Daddy said, "everyone seemed quite upset." Looking out of his window, he saw the hip of a huge horse and as his eyes rose, he could see a fully uniformed policeman staring down at him. "Have you been drinking?" asked the officer. "No," replied Daddy, "we're not from around here." "And just where are you from, son?" asked the officer. "Heath Springs," said Daddy, beaming with pride. The officer had heard enough and instructed them to turn around right there in the middle of the street and to follow him. They slowly progressed down the street, turning left at the next intersection, where they soon came to a sign that read PARKING. "How long are you boys going to be in the city," asked the officer? "Three days, unless we run out of money," said Daddy. "Well, park it in there and don't get it out until you are ready to go home, and it will be in less than three days." He was right, as by the next afternoon they were on their way back to South Carolina. They had failed to set aside enough funds for parking.

The Junk Yard Dog

On a road trip to New Orleans, Randy and I stopped in Pascagoula, Mississippi for a bathroom break. Several old men watched as one of them handed me the key and said, "Its right around back." The men's and lady's bathrooms were side by side separated by a cinder block wall about 4 feet high. The wall extended out and formed the shape of a T. When I exited the bathroom, the door locked behind me and right there was the biggest/meanest German Shephard I had ever seen. He was coming for me, and all I could do was jump over that wall. He came around the T so I jumped back over. After doing this several times, I realized I had to make a run for it so the next time he came around the T, I waited until the last possible second—jumped over and took off. I made it about 10 feet before he caught me, knocked me down and was chewing on my butt. Frantically crawling, I made it to the corner of the building where his chain stopped him. Looking up, there stood the old men; and one of them said, "If you hadn't slipped when you started running, you might have made it." Another man said, "You did better than that boy yesterday." Now I know what retired men do for entertainment in Mississippi.

James Gets a Star

I learned about the power of motivation when I coached an eleven and twelve year old football team. The boys were told that if they blocked a punt, intercepted a pass, or recovered a fumble, that I would paint a star on their helmet. James' eyes grew to the size of moon pies. "How big will the star be," he asked, "what color will it be—will it be on the front or back?" "James," I said, "first you've got to accomplish one of those three things. You do that and then we will talk." James was oblivious. "But I need to know where on my helmet the star will be!" "JAMES, I will put it anywhere you want—just get out there," I shouted. On the ensuing kickoff, James sprinted down the field like a mad man possessed, not only making the tackle but also causing a fumble which he recovered. He came off the field holding his helmet and pointing to its' left front. "I want my star right here," he said.

You've Got to Know
When to Fold Them

Every Thursday night of my life, between the ages of 23 and 30, we played poker. We played games like Queens And, Baseball, In Between, and High-Low Chicago. About the most anyone ever won or lost was 50 dollars, but that proved to be a good entertainment value considering that we would play all night. The rear door to Billy's trailer had no outside steps, and it was about a two foot drop from the threshold to the ground. When a new player needed a bathroom break, he was directed right that way, and you can guess what would happen. No limbs were ever broken, however, many funny bones were fractured.

A Thief in the Night

Some of our poker games were held at Benny's house right there in the middle of Heath Springs. Often there was loud music, loud laughter, and loud everything and although the neighbors grumbled from time to time they never formally complained. The game usually broke up around 3am and during the wintertime, on his way home; Peter would swing by the Heath Springs Mercantile to pick up some coal for his fireplace. The coal pile was located about 50 feet from the police station, and in Peter's mind this was perfect. His reasoning was that no one would believe that anyone would steal anything from so close to the jail, and he was right. Peter had discovered a coal mine, and monetarily the outcome of the game was of little consequence because win, lose, or draw he would be warm for the next week.

Benny Leaves His Mark

One Saturday night after some serious partying in Camden, Benny was making his way home when all of a sudden there was a blue light in his rear view mirror, and it wasn't long before he became a guest of Kershaw County for the evening. As he sat on the concrete slab which now was his bed, he pondered his three charges and 168.00 dollar predicament. It was then, on the wall, he noticed numerous pearls of wisdom and initials left by former residents. Not to be outdone, Benny removed his belt and with the buckle began to leave his own mark. Looking up he noticed a county officer scribbling on his pad. "That's another 34.00 dollars" the policeman said, "defacing county property."

Weasel's Place

One Saturday night, we were looking for some excitement so we decided to stop by Weasel's Place. This was a real Honky Tonk located in Bone Town. The structure was a simple cinder block building, but inside you could find all the trappings of a country Hot Spot—cold beer, music, and a bathroom for the ladies. There was no lot for parking so people just left their cars along the roadside which didn't sit well with the authorities and soon the county police installed NO PARKING signs. According to Weasel, some of the local teenagers spray painted over the NO, so now they just read PARKING. The county had recently declared Weasel's Place not only a menace, but also a danger to the community—which increased patronage by 50 percent. As we sat in the car deciding when to go in, a man came backing out of the door and was immediately struck by a woman wielding a pool cue. It was that kind of place. On the inside, in one corner was Lloyd's mat on which lay who else but Lloyd. He was weaving in and out of consciousness and when I came into focus he said, "I just want to tell you one thing." I waited and again he said, "I just want to tell you one thing." That was what he said to everybody, "I just want to tell you one thing." About every thirty minutes someone would check to see if Lloyd was still among the living, and he would say, "I just want to tell you one thing." At about 1am a crowd gathered and pressed Lloyd to tell us the one thing. Someone unplugged the boom box, and the entire place fell silent awaiting Lloyd's words of wisdom. Lloyd raised his finger and said, "I just want to tell you one thing. . . .

I like a woman with tall hair." "What?" exclaimed Hazel. "Is that it—Is that the one thing? Hell, we all like women with tall hair!" Lloyd's big moment had been a bust and soon Weasel's Place would be busted out of business as well. The county stepped up their efforts to force closure by manning a license check at the nearby crossroads and stopping people as they departed. Since everybody was guilty of something and most had warrants, this proved effective on all but the hard core. Finally the Sheriff's Office had the power cut off, and that was the end of Weasel's Place. Not long after that, women wearing tall hair went out of style too!

I Love My Job

Not long after graduating from the Citadel, I became employed with the South Carolina Employment Security Commission as a youth counselor. Pretty soon the program was booming, and it became necessary for me to have an assistant. My boss informed me that a candidate had been selected, and moreover, that she was a friend of our Executive Director's daughter. This was cause for some concern, however upon my first sighting of Libby, I quickly determined that she was qualified. We were married several years later and have been now for over thirty two years. It's nice when you enjoy your work.

Some things you just can't put into words. . . .

Love Hurts

When I took Libby to meet Mr. Pum and Granny, they were both in their eighties; and both exhibiting health problems—Mr. Pum with hearing and Granny with mobility. "Championship Wrestling" was on TV, and so loud that we could hear it clearly from the yard. Knocking on the door was useless so I walked down the long porch until I got to their living room window, where I could see Granny sitting up in bed; and Mr. Pum was sitting in his chair beside her, only about two feet away. Granny saw us but could not speak loud enough (over the TV) to get his attention. She gave me that "wait a minute" signal as she slowly scanned the bed for her *Life* magazine. Methodically and purposely she rolled it lengthwise and WHAM. She wacked Mr. Pum with all of the strength she could muster. He reacted with surprise and looked at her as if she had lost her mind, however, she now had his attention and pointed to the window where Libby and I stood watching. Although in a loving relationship, their primary means of communication now depended on violent physical contact—they did what they had to do.

Beware the Goose

Shelter Rock Lake covers about four acres, with almost one acre considered as wet lands—swamp. There is a narrow strip of land in the upper end extending out almost to the middle, and it is a good spot for fishing or viewing wildlife. One evening I was showing it to Libby, when we noticed a large goose swimming methodically back and forth, never leaving the area. "Be still," I said, "I think he is going to come over here." He just continued swimming back and forth until I noticed at my feet the female goose sitting on her nest. He knew that we had not seen her, but as soon as we did, he knew that too. Now he was coming for us, and he was serious. "Run," I shouted, grabbing Libby by the hand. He chased us about twenty yards flapping his wings and squawking to high heaven. About two months later, we saw the proud parent with eight babies cruising the lake, however, this time I made sure not to get too close.

No Scalp Zone

In 1992, we were living in Rock Hill. I was scanning my Saturday morning paper, when to my surprise; I read that Pep was pitching that night for the California Angels against the Baltimore Orioles in Baltimore. I had known Pep for many years and used to carry him and his Dixie Boys teammates to the Dairy Queen in the back of my truck. The Angels and Orioles were both many games behind in the standings so a ticket should not be a problem, if only we could get a flight. We did and arrived in Baltimore about 4 pm, where we got a car and drove straight to the ball park. To my shock and bewilderment, the sign on the ticket window said SOLD OUT. "How can this be?" I asked. "It's August 24th," the ticket agent said, "Cal Ripken's birthday and this game sold out six days before the season began." All of a sudden I began to feel sick. After pleading my dilemma, she directed us to the "No Scalp Zone" where you might be able to score tickets—we were number 22 for 2. Luckily we got seats, and Pep did great. That was a special night, watching a hometown kid pitching in the Majors, not to mention our ticket adventure.

Ugly Works for Me

Sometimes in life, a little forward thinking can prove to be a valuable thing. At about the time Libby's children were approaching driving age, we were in need of a car. Plyler's Used Cars had a reputation for stocking reliable but low priced vehicles, and there I found a 1983 Mercury that was so ugly, flies wouldn't light on it. During a test drive, I found in the glove box, the phone number of the previous owner—turned out to be an older gentleman living in Florida. "Don't buy that car son. It's a lemon," he said. "The floor mats don't fit, the back window will not roll down, and the carpet is coming loose in the trunk." "What about the mechanical aspects, such as the motor and transmission," I asked, "any problems there?" "No all that stuff works fine," he said, "but I'm advising you not to buy it—it's a lemon." I bought it, and sure enough, the kids were ashamed to be seen in it, much less wanting to drive it. It, however like I suspected, was a good car and lasted until we were able to step up to a Honda.

Speed Racer

For my fortieth birthday, Libby gave me a Richard Petty Driving Experience. It was expensive and on the way to Charlotte, my concern was that there would be a huge emphasis on safety and that they would be saying "be careful—drive safely—don't go to fast," etc. As the time neared for me to begin, it became evident that no one showed any concern for my safety or my survival, to the contrary, it was emphasized that if I did not go fast enough, the procession would be stopped so faster drivers could be moved to the front. Additionally, right before starting, a guy sticks his head in my car and says, "Oh yeah, in case of fire, pull that pin to the right of your seat." "What pin!" I exclaimed. "Where and why might there be a fire?" "Don't worry," the guy says, "we've only had one serious accident since I've been here." By now, my thinking has shifted from worrying about getting my money's worth to worrying about living to see another birthday. I made eight laps with a top speed of 132 MPH, however, that was not nearly as fast as my heart was beating. I learned one thing that day—that driving a race car is not as easy as it looks on TV. When I came in from my last lap, my fingers were embedded in the steering wheel like John Candy's in *Planes, Trains, and Automobiles,* and I had strained a muscle in my neck from the clenching so tightly. The guy said that I did pretty well for a rookie, which seemed to help my neck a little, however, I still have trouble opening my hands all the way.

The Kidney Stone

Libby and I were living in Rock Hill when I decided to go for a ride on my motorcycle. Passing through Great Falls my mid-section began to hurt and by the time I arrived home, the pain was almost unbearable. Having endured a kidney stone in the past I was familiar with the drill, and knew the time had come to visit the hospital. As I entered the emergency room doors, I could see several people in line talking to the receptionist and not wanting to appear as a wimp, I waited my turn. In about ten minutes, she asked why I was there. "Kidney stone," I said, gritting my teeth. "Are you in pain?" she asked. "I passed the pain stage about an hour ago—now it's more like agony," I replied, still gritting my teeth. She said that some paperwork must be completed before admission. "My names is James M. Horton, and I live at 1927 Wellford Woods Lane." "Wellford Woods?" she inquired. "My cousin lives in Wellford Woods. Do you like it out there?" As you can imagine, our relationship went downhill from there. However, as a result of my reply to her, I received expedited treatment. It's hard to be nice when one is suffering.

Shake Your Money Maker

One summer Libby and I decided to take a Caribbean cruise with Phoebe and Bob, her sister and brother-in-law. Departing Fort Lauderdale, our sights were set on the Lesser Antilles of the Eastern Caribbean and specifically the island of Antigua. Upon arrival we were excited about our previously planned excursion, which was a trip along the coastline aboard an authentic pirate ship and culminating with a visit to a secluded beach where we could enter the water via rope swing. Booked mostly by young people, the tour included plenty of loud music and dancing as well as unlimited rum punch. During the adventure, Libby became concerned that Phoebe was not having a good time amidst all the alcohol and sordid activities; moreover, Libby feared that she may be harboring some hard feelings after finding herself in these uncomfortable surroundings. "I don't think Phoebe is enjoying herself," she said. "She prefers a more demure atmosphere—please go and make sure that she is not upset." Scanning the deck, I could see the tail end of the conga line disappearing behind the rear of the ship and as the dancers snaked through the galley and reemerged on the side deck, who is leading the procession but Phoebe. She had a rum punch in her left hand while simultaneously twirling her right index finger in the air. "This dum runch is good and contains no alcohol," she said. "I'm having my third one." Libby was speechless, and I will forever regret not being able to locate my camera.

Bad Chicken

One summer, Libby and I were cleaning out the freezer when we discovered some frozen chicken that was several years old—we decided to get rid of it. Libby put it in our trash bin for pick up; however, after several days the men had not come and with the temperature reaching 100 degrees daily, we began to notice an unpleasant odor. I knew what it was and decided to get rid of it the next day. That night I received a call regarding an emergency at work, which turned out to be an issue taking the entire day to resolve and by the time I got home, the smell had progressed from unpleasant to choking. It was so bad the cats would not come out of the garage. Something would have to be done tomorrow, and Libby would have to participate since it was her decision to throw it out in the first place. Wearing one glove and holding my nose with the other hand, I managed to throw it in the back of my truck but where to take it? Columbia is not like the country, so after much deliberation, we decided on the Kershaw County convenience site as our best solution, so down Two Notch Road we headed. At the first stop light, the people in the car beside us began gagging and quickly rolled up their windows. At the second light, someone mentioned a dead body before speeding off. Ya'll, it was bad! Even people walking down the sidewalk were coughing and waving their hands in an effort to locate breathable air. By the time we arrived at the convenience site, I had my doubts whether we would be allowed to make the drop. "I've got some bad chicken," I told the man at the gate. He never flinched as he pointed to one of the containers. I guess he had smelled unpleasantness before, or maybe his nose didn't work but anyway, we got rid of the bad chicken and got a good laugh in the process.

All in a Day's Work

Let me say a few words about retirement. When I was working, my life was hectic—so many obligations and never enough time. Since retirement, waiting in line is no problem, and talking to telemarketers is a pleasure. Most things can be delayed or put off indefinitely; however, I do enjoy writing short stories, but I don't even have to finish them if I don't want. . . .